Tackle Fencing

Tackle Fencing

AN INTRODUCTION TO THE FOIL

Bob Anderson

Stanley Paul, London

Stanley Paul & Co Ltd
3 Fitzroy Square, London W1P 6JD

An imprint of the Hutchinson Publishing Group

London Melbourne Sydney Auckland
Wellington Johannesburg and agencies
throughout the world

First published 1970 as *All About Fencing*
This edition 1978

Printed in Great Britain
at The Anchor Press Ltd and bound by
Wm Brendon & Son Ltd
both of Tiptree, Essex

ISBN 0 09 131220 5 cased
     0 09 131221 3 paperback

CONTENTS

FOREWORD

Fencing is a sport of perception and intuition as well as one of technique. This book explores both areas and tries to explain the sport *as a whole*. It is nowhere near being a comprehensive technical manual – only the fundamentals are covered, but they are covered fully.

Fencing is essentially an "open" skill, where the perfection of technique can be seen as a means to an end – to defeat an opponent. Therefore you should not think that following the practical advice and mastering the handful of essential movements described will ensure that you fence well. My purpose is not primarily to teach you how to plan your game but is to help you understand the relationship between technique and intuition. You must then develop your own individual game in the light of this understanding.

As will be seen, in emphasising intuition I have no wish to denigrate technique – some fencers succeed very largely because of excellent technique. But others, who possess high intuitive perception and a fine sense of pace and distance, can succeed without a high technical standard. (This premium on intuition is partly why women can compete on equal terms with men, though the observation should not be thought to suggest that their technique is necessarily inferior.)

What type of fencer you are will not only depend on the degree to which you possess these abilities but also on your own motivational factor – what you want to get out of the game. Are you one who delights in the precision of technique, in the joy of performing a movement sweetly and masterfully, or are you one who wishes primarily to win and see technique *only* as a means to this end? The top competitive fencer must possess both fine technique and a high desire to win. But such people are born, not made. What *you* must do is understand your own motivation and develop your game in accordance with it. Not only will you thus enjoy it more but you will realise also your maximum potential. This is a point which I believe is too much overlooked. Clearly the approach of the club coach and the attitudes of other club members is of influence here but, nevertheless, each fencer, if he wishes to do the best that is in him, owes it to himself to take account of his own motives. This will be the strongest influence on his performance and his success in competition.

The book covers foil fencing only. You would be ill-advised to start with the épée or the sabre, not primarily because they are more difficult or less interesting but because foil fencers outnumber the others by about ten to one, and because foil is suitable for both sexes, whereas only men can cope with the other blades. There is little point in turning up at your club for an evening's fencing only to find there is no-one with whom you can fence sabre. Moreover, only very large clubs run beginner classes in épée and sabre.

BOB ANDERSON

1 What is fencing all about?

The more you understand fencing, the more you will enjoy it. This particularly applies to the novice for, like all highly skilled games, it is easy to be put off by the chore of having to begin right at the beginning.

I will start with a little bit of history, not for its own sake but because it can be the beginning of understanding. The foil evolved from the Italian *floretta*, a light, practice sword, which was used in the fencing *salle* up to the eighteenth century to rehearse the movements used in the duel; the duelling sword was too dangerous for this. Duels were indeed frequent and training in swordmanship a real necessity for a man of breeding if he wished to survive. At practice the fighter was urged to hit where the vital organs lie and thus the target area for the kill was the trunk. In foil fencing today we talk of a hit "on target" and a hit "off target" and our target area is much the same as in those deadly serious sword schools.

But what went on then and what goes on now bear little resemblance. To us, used to the complex brilliance of modern foil fencing, the limited sword play would strike us as dull and the caution of their approach would surprise us. Outside the fencing salle, where they put their learning to its deadly purpose, the proceedings were even slower and more careful. And naturally so – with your life at stake you don't try dazzling sword play – you wait, watch for that momentary lapse in concentration and make your sudden lunge. With no room for mistakes there is no room for experiment. The more movements you make the more chance there is of being hit.

With the growth of fire arms, the sword lost its supremacy as the weapon of death. If challenged you could always opt for duelling pistols. Now, therefore, you could go to a fencing master for fun and afford to learn risky manoeuvres. When, in 1780, the mask to protect the face was introduced and risk to the eyes eliminated, there remained no restriction, by motivation or safety concern, to the development of what became called a *conversation with the blade* – the modern game of fencing had arrived.

I say all this to emphasise that fencing is a *game* and to give perspective to the rules or conventions by which foil fencing is played. The conventions have been adopted to encourage this conversation with the blade – without them the game will be chaotic and dull. Simply to give people foils, masks and protective jacket and require them to fight is rather like giving two people tennis rackets and balls, putting them in the middle of a rough field without a net or side lines and expecting them to play tennis.

Sequence 1

FIRST COUNTER RIPOSTE

This occupies the first two sequences
which are continuous. See p. 33

Sequence 2

FIRST COUNTER RIPOSTE

continued

Sequence 3

THE LATERAL PARRY

See p. 61

Sequence 4

THE SEMI-CIRCULAR PARRY

See p. 62

Sequence 5

THE CIRCULAR PARRY

See p. 61

See page 94 for start of sequences 6 to 10

Why do we have conventions in foil fencing?

What are the main foil conventions and what are their function? Firstly, the target area is limited to the trunk and excludes the arms, legs and head. A fencing rally, or *phrase* as it is called, ends, provided no other rules have been broken, with a hit, either on or off target. If on, then a point is scored. You can see, therefore, that one accurate hit on target is worth more than a hundred hits on the arm or the mask. Furthermore (and one can almost hear the old masters drilling this into their earnest pupils) a hit must be made with the point, clearly and distinctly and with such effect that the blade would penetrate, were the sword sharp (see any of the sequence pictures where a hit is scored); you must not graze or scrape the target with the point. The result is that any careless jab is unlikely to result in a scoring hit.

Now these limitations on how you score do not, as you might think, cramp the play. Particularly as a beginner, you will find that they liberate it by enabling you to concentrate on doing certain things without fearing totally unsuspected approaches by your opponent. Neither do the restrictions necessarily shorten the fencing phrase. To take up our tennis analogy, rallies would not last long if the purpose was just to hit the ball past your opponent, without regard for it being inside or outside the court and if the ball could come through at any height, even along the ground.

12

A second important convention: if A tries to hit B and if B defends himself by deflecting aside the point of the attacking sword with a parry, then the right to attack, or *riposte*, passes to B. If A parries B's riposte – B's attempt to hit him – then the right to attack returns to A who then makes a further riposte, or counter riposte. And so a fencing phrase continues until either a hit (valid or invalid) is made or one of the few other rules is infringed (e.g. if bodies touch, called *corps-à-corps*, the French for "body to body"). See here the sequence pictures for the First Counter Riposte, numbers 1 and 2, to see the general pattern. *N.B. A counter riposte is really the same as a riposte. All ripostes after the first are called counter ripostes.*

Back to tennis, and this time on a traditional court – you can see that a fencing phrase resembles a tennis rally, with the attack passing from fencer to fencer as the ball goes back and forth over the net. Take the respective conventions away and the fencing will resemble tennis played with two balls – one to each player – who will be required to attack and defend at the same time – hitting their own ball and preparing to receive their opponent's. It *might* be possible but rallies would certainly be short and ragged.*

*The analogy is not exact–whereas tennis so conceived is not played and is hardly playable, fencing without the foil conventions is possible and is indeed played – with the épée. Here there is no right of riposte and the target is the whole body, down to the hands and feet. With such
(*See over*)

The foil conventions, therefore, have been devised to make the game better *as a game* and they are in particular of great benefit to the beginner since they help him channel his effort, they help him begin at the beginning.

Fencing as "physical chess"

I have used the analogy with tennis – another close and revealing analogy is with chess. Fencing has been described as physical chess, without a checkmate. The essence of chess is the ability to anticipate and intercept the opponent's play, be it in attack or defence. You do this by probing his defences, seeking out how he reacts to your moves and anticipating from what he has done in the past to what he will do in the future. You lay traps for him, deceive him as to your intention, make inspired guesses about how he will react, play cat and mouse with him, feed invitations to him to commit himself to an attack. You try to think a move or so ahead of your opponent, you vary your play with each opponent. And, all the time, your opponent is probing and testing you in return. This is a description of chess and, perhaps more

vulnerability and where anything goes to a certain degree, épée is a more cautious weapon for the beginner – he cannot experiment or take chances. Épée fencing derives, in fact, from duelling proper and resembles very closely the later, more formal period of duelling where you fought "to first blood" rather than to death. A hit on the hand would be "first blood", the duel would end, honour was satisfied.

14

than any other physical game or sport, this is a description of fencing also.

Now I want to emphasise to you that it is the restricted field of play, the essential simplicity of the basic fencing phrase – attack, parry and riposte, parry and counter riposte, etc., that give this quality to fencing. They are the physical equivalent of the board on which chess is played. What they do, in effect, is to bring prominently into the game two elements which would otherwise be of lesser importance – mental agility and technical speed. Without these the only major quality for success would be sheer physical speed.

Now a fencer can outwit another, guess which move the opponent will make when it is his turn, be prepared for it and base his counter riposte to take advantage of where he expects his opponent to parry – and deceive it; he can tempt his opponent into making a certain riposte, being prepared for this type of move and parrying it in a certain way so that his own counter riposte can be that much more effective. Fencing is a game of deception – there is far more joy in outwitting an opponent of comparable physical speed and technical skill than there is in defeating him *simply* because you can move faster than he.

Technical speed is brought to prominence, as opposed to sheer physical speed, by the fact that, as it were, you take turns to move. This applies particularly to the beginner, where the variety of moves he can make is limited since he has only learnt a few. If his moves are to be effective, they

must be properly, quickly and accurately made. His opponent knows that the riposte will be one of the four, say, which are commonly known to both of them. If the riposte is technically slow, i.e. clumsy and inaccurate, he will have time to defend himself even if he does not know which of the four it will be. You can deceive an opponent as to what you are going to do but then lose so much time in making the riposte that he parries successfully. This is not a question of physical speed – it is more analogous to the fact that the shortest distance between two points is a straight line. If you move in a circle where you should move in a straight line, you may be too late no matter how fast you actually move.

Advice for the beginner

Even though fencing is a technical game, I hope it is now clear that the beginner should not be deterred, when he first arrives at a club, by the seemingly amazing agility and speed of reaction of the most experienced players. I believe, and it is basic to this book, that a learner can begin to fence, rather than practice movements, virtually straight away. He will very quickly pick up the essential structure of the game and the part which both deception and technical speed play in it. Once he has grasped these and applied himself to them, he is in a position to fence, i.e. fight. Right from the beginning he can be in a position to score hits; he can begin quickly to try to deceive his opponent. Technically he may and will be woefully inadequate but he will already be on the learning trail.

As a beginner, going along to a club, you also will probably want to play the game as soon as possible, to get the general impression and feel of moving with the sword in your hand. I hope, therefore, you are not made to tackle the game solely from the technical aspect. In the past fencing has been treated as a mystique rather than a healthy sport involving a lot of physical exercise and an alert mental approach. From the technical angle, fencing is a difficult game to get into but fortunately it is not just technique – it is technique plus the ability to put it into practice in competition. Whatever your technical level, therefore, the deception which is so fundamental to the game should enable you to enjoy it.

All I want to do in this book is set you firmly into the learning process and discuss fully the elements of the game upon which all the rest is based. I shall be concerned with *what* is required and *when*, rather than too much *how* it is done. I want you to get into the game as soon as possible and, to this end, I will tend to treat the basic moves, etc., as they apply in a fight situation, not as applied in a fencing syllabus.

The process of learning

What is the learning process as it applies to beginners, and why am I talking about this before I have described the movements

17

with which it is concerned? The reasons are that, like the beginner at his club, I want you to understand what learning to fence is all about and also that I wish to avoid the suggestion that there must be an absolutely fixed syllabus for learning – a fixed progression from one movement to another. I do not deny that there is such a pattern – most people do, in fact, learn in a certain order. But there is no necessity. I want you to think of the moves you will be learning as arising naturally in a fight situation. The following, fictional, oversimplified story will serve as example to what I mean.

Two novices, Bob and Ken, come to a coach and say, "I want to fence". The coach gives them masks, jackets and foils and, having explained where and how they must hit to score, sends them off to get on with it. They soon find that he who attacks first always strikes home and they get bored. The coach then points out that they are standing too close, that their reaction times are not fast enough, so that when Bob attacks, Ken simply has not enough time to parry him. They then stand further apart and now find that they give each other such warning that when one attacks the other also has time to attack and that they hit each other simultaneously. Again they get bored, so the coach shows Bob that if he stretches forward quickly and extends his arm absolutely straight, almost at the same time, he will always hit, because his reach is greater than Ken's (who doesn't stretch, in any case).

Now Bob always wins these battles, so

18

Ken realises he cannot attack but must defend. By keeping well away he has time to see Bob lunge and to parry it aside, from right to left, deflecting it aside from the target. Now again there is stalemate, until the coach points out to Ken that Bob's lunge has brought him well within range and that if he parries so that the opposing point is clear, he can hit Bob if he immediately ripostes, for Bob has not been taught to parry. The game is boring again for scoring still seems a matter of chance and speed.

The coach takes Bob aside and suggests that he make a feint, that he pretend to attack as usual with his blade to the right of Ken's. When Ken parries from right to left, Bob can move his blade underneath, in the opposite direction, and then attack to the sword-arm side, over Ken's sword-arm in fact.

Now we come, in this history, to a crucial moment. Although Bob does all this he finds that repeatedly his point catches on Ken's sword arm. At this point the coach has to say, "Look, you must now learn some technique, because there's a limit to just doing what comes naturally. Up till now I have been teaching you what to do and why to do it. Now you must learn *how* to do it."

Let us take stock of the situation. There are three points:

First: real life is unlikely to be so neat and orderly as that but, however it goes, sooner or later the novice must ask *how?* and not *what?*

19

Second: there is no mystery at all. It started with two novices just prodding at each other in the most clumsy fashion and progressed from there, one thing naturally leading to another.

Third: other than the target area and the correct way to hit, none of the conventions of foil fencing have been mentioned. The advice given has solely been with the purpose of lubricating the game for the beginner, helping him to enjoy it.

The absence of talk about conventions demonstrates that they are neither mysterious nor hampering. They are the rails on which the game is played, laid down so that it moves smoothly and naturally. In the same way, as you learn to fence, so will you adopt the classic stance and patterns of rather ritualistic behaviour which can bemuse the beginner. You will adopt them naturally, as you learn.

The situation I have outlined above resembles the sort of process which I personally think the most enjoyable and in the best interests of the fencer. I think the novice who is encouraged to come back to the coach and say, "Look, I'm getting bored with this constant prodding – there must be more to the game. What have I got to learn – every time I attack him, he does something and I can't hit him?", will enjoy his fencing more than the fencer who learns in isolation, outside a fight situation, how to parry and riposte, counter riposte and counter attack – without knowing why he has to learn it.

What is more, it should be clear that he

will only learn fencing as a whole by being in the fight situation. He will be trying to frustrate his opponent and he will be told either to do something else or to do something, which he is doing, quicker and better. And the real point is that sooner or later, he will have to do something *better*. He will only know he must do it better because his present efforts are failing.

It is well to understand from the beginning that to learn fencing is to learn technique. Now I hold no brief for technique as such. John Jacobs, in his companion volume to this on golf, *Play Better Golf*, points out that golf is a game of "how many?" and not "how?". People may often be interested in *what* you score, but rarely in how you did it. A simple but true comment on any competitive game and particularly relevant to fencing, where technique can be of obsessive interest. Such absorption is fine but it should not obscure that technique is a means to an end, which is to score hits on an opponent in competition. It is what you do and when you do it as much as how you do it.

But the technique must be there. Your movements and stance must approximate to the standard laid down as the classical style over the years. There will be variations between fencers, for there is no point in adopting a style which you personally feel to be awkward and uncomfortable – the standard must be adapted to each person's physique. But it must be there.

21

2 The structure of the game

Lefthanders: for instruction it is immaterial whether a fencer is right or left handed. The position of the sword hand and the nature of each parry is related to the fencer in question, not to a sort of fixed guide. The left-hander is a mirror image of the right-hander, with the sixte position and parry still on the sword-arm side.

On guard and ready to fence

The objective of foil fencing is to score the required number of hits with the point of the sword on the opponent's target within a specified time limit: five hits in six minutes for men, four hits in five minutes for women is the competitive structure. The target for men and women is virtually the trunk of the body, excluding the legs, the arms and the head (see fig. 1). The competitive game is played within the confines of a strip, called the *piste*, 14 metres long and two metres wide.

Fencers face each other in the *on guard* position, which is not a natural one and requires considerable practice. The knees are bent and the sword arm is held forward, bent, with the hand at breast level. The blade can obviously point up or down and the hand can be held out in front of you either to the right or left (see beginnings of sequence pictures 8 and 6 for illustration

22

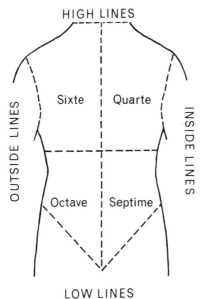

HIGH LINES

Sixte | Quarte

OUTSIDE LINES

INSIDE LINES

Octave | Septime

LOW LINES

Lines of the target   *Fig. 1*
*Sixte and Quarte are known as the high lines
and Octave and Septime as the low lines.
Sixte and Octave are known as the outside
lines, and Quarte and Septime as the inside
lines.*
This is for a right-handed fencer.

of right and left respectively). There are
eight on-guard positions. This book will
deal in detail with only two of them, not
primarily because the others are more complicated or less important, but to simplify
the discussion of the subsequent moves in
the game. We will either be on guard in
sixte or in *quarte*. These names refer back
finally to two of the four simple parries
which are fundamental to the game. They

23

are all the same sort of simple parry but the hand and blade are orientated differently for each. The target itself is divided into theoretical lines named after these parries, which are designed to protect them (see fig. 1). When on guard in sixte the sword hand is placed so as to cover and protect the area so marked.

Both fencers stand at such a distance that they cannot hit the target without extending the sword arm and lunging forward – this is called *fencing measure* and much tactic is concerned with deceiving your opponent as to whether he is or is not within hitting distance. They can either fence with *engagement of blade* or with *absence of blade*. These refer respectively to whether the blades are or are not touching each other. We will deal in detail only with fencing with blades engaged (i.e. crossing, in contact), because this leads on more directly to the basic attacks and parries with which we are concerned. Blades, for our purpose, can be *engaged in sixte* or *engaged in quarte*.

Technically these refer to the side of the blade they are engaged on. There is no need to bother about why they are so called – remember that if you are engaged so that the outside of the blades are in contact, you are engaged in sixte, and if the inside of the blades are in contact you are engaged in quarte. Inside and outside refer to the lines of the target. The outside lines are those on the sword arm side, the inside those away from the sword arm. (See fig. 1 for the target lines and figs. 3z and 3x, p. 28,

24

for engagements in sixte and quarte respectively.)

The direct attack/being covered and uncovered

Attacks can be launched from either of the engaged positions. The simplest form of attack is the direct attack. This consists, quite simply, of straightening the arm from whichever engagement you are in, followed immediately by a lunge. (We have no sequential pictures of the direct attack as such, but the second and third offensive movements from sequences 1 and 2, the first counter riposte, are direct ripostes. There you can see the direct movement of the blades toward the target.)

If you are engaged in quarte you attack *into the line* of quarte, and similarly with sixte. Now before discussing how to stop this attack, we must consider the situation a little more closely, for it is the danger of such an attack from the engaged position and the attempts to stop such an attack from even developing which are the starting point for all that follows. Look now at the accompanying pictures A and B of fig. 2. In A the fencers are engaged down the *line of fence*, an imaginary line drawn through both fencers when on guard facing each other; they are engaged in the middle of the target. You can see that the far fencer can be hit on both sides of his blade (assuming that he keeps it still) – he can be hit direct in the line of quarte and he can also be hit in the line of sixte by the

25

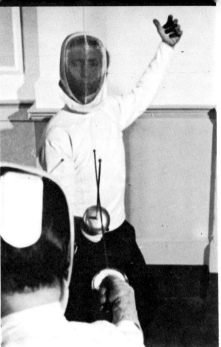

A   Engaged in quarte   *Fig. 2*

attacker moving his blade into the other line and attacking with an *indirect attack*. If you look at picture B, on the other hand, you will see that he cannot be hit on target by a direct attack – he can only be hit by an indirect attack, round the other side of his blade.

In the nature of things engagements tend to be in the middle of the target, down the line of fence, where both fencers (for what applies to one clearly applies to the other) can be attacked on both sides of the blade, or where they are *uncovered* in both lines. Now being uncovered in both lines, liable to both a direct attack and an indirect

B Engaged in quarte   *Fig. 2*

attack, is clearly uncomfortable and un-pleasant, and fencers therefore try to cover themselves in such a way that they can only be attacked by indirect attack. That is, they try to avoid being in position A and like to be in position B.

A fencer attempts to cover himself by lateral movements of his blade, i.e. by *pushing* the opposing blade across, or by changing his engagement from one line to the other (e.g. from quarte to sixte). The value and purpose of the change of engage-ment is as follows. Should you find your-self in the position of the fencer with back to camera in B, unable to attack direct and

X (above) Y (below)   *Fig. 3*

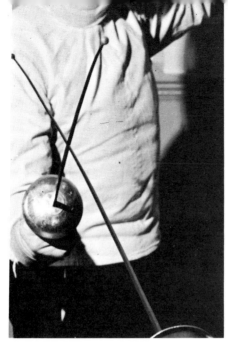

Z   *Fig. 3*

therefore himself vulnerable to a direct
attack,* you can alter the picture completely by moving your blade around below
and engaging in the other line (see fig. 3:
quarte in X, around in Y to quarte in Z).
Then you will be covered and the opponent
will be uncovered.

---

*Think about his position. It is clear that if one
fencer is covered in a line of engagement, then
the other fencer *must* be uncovered. There are
no two ways about this. If, as in A, both fencers
are engaged down the line of fence then, of
course, both are uncovered to a direct attack
and therefore both can also score hits with a
direct attack. But in B, where one is covered
in the direct line, the other must be uncovered.

Now these attempts of a fencer to cover himself, attempts which he must make if he is to be safe from a direct attack are, paradoxically, the stimuli for all the indirect attacks to which I will now refer in more detail. There are three of them – the *disengage*, the *cut-over* and the *counter disengage*. Look now at sequence 6 for the cut-over, sequence 7 for the counter disengage, and the opening of sequence 3 for the disengage.

They are called indirect attacks because the final lunge is preceded in each case by a preliminary blade movement. Without commenting on them in detail at this stage, you can see that the disengage involves passing the blade under the opponent's and then lunging into the opposite line (in this case, moving from quarte into sixte); the cut-over also involves moving the blade from one line to another, but in this case it is done by withdrawing it so that it passes over the top of the opponent's blade (we will leave the counter disengage for a moment).

The stimuli for these attacks is quite simple. If your opponent puts lateral pressure on your blade and at the same time you remove it by cut-over or disengage, his blade will continue to move in its original direction, while your blade moves into the opposite line, where he is uncovered. If, on the other hand, your opponent tries to cover himself by a change of guard, you deceive him by following his blade round with your own. This is the indirect attack by counter disengage – look carefully at

30

sequence 7, and you will see this; note that whereas attacks by disengage and cut-over end in the opposite line, the attack by counter disengage ends in the same line of engagement.

Defence

I have not mentioned defence so far not because it is less important (indeed, fencing has been called the art of defence), but because an attack always precedes defence and I think it important that you understand how attacks start.

There are three basic parries which you must master as a beginner – the simple or lateral parry, the semi-circular or low-line parry and the circular or counter parry. (I will stick to the more easily recognizable name which best describe the action – lateral, circular and semi-circular.) Look at sequences 3, 4, and 5.

The lateral parry (sequence 3) is here used on a disengage attack from sixte to quarte – the hand and blade moving across from right to left in a lateral motion. The thicker, stronger part of your blade (the *forte*) connects with the thinner, weaker part of the attacking blade (the *foible*) and carries it away across the quarte line. This is the *lateral parry of quarte* – it is so called because it parries an attack from away to the outside the quarte line of the target. Were it to move from left to right, parrying the attack from the right breast (line of sixte) beyond the sword arm, it would be called a lateral parry of sixte. As a rule to remem-

31

ber – a parry is called after the line it defends.

The circular parry (sequence 5) is here used on a disengage attack from quarte to sixte. The parrying blade describes a circle in an anticlockwise direction, passing under the attacking blade as it advances and collecting it as the circle is completed, bringing the blades back into the original line of engagement. This is a *circular parry of quarte*. Taken in the sixte line it would move in a clockwise direction.

The *semi-circular parry* (sequence 4) is here used on a disengage attack from sixte into quarte. The point of the blade describes a semi-circular anticlockwise inward from the sixte position, over the top of the attacking blade, deflecting it downward and away into the low line, into the line of octave. This is the *semi-circular parry of octave*. Taken from the quarte line this parry would move clockwise inward and downward into the line of septime.*

You will find yourself varying your

---

*This is the first mention I have made of the low lines of octave and septime. The low lines refer to the part of the target visible under the opposing sword arm, the high lines refer to those visible over the sword arm. The lines of quarte and sixte are those we have been concerned with in the high line. In the low line *octave* is directly below sixte, and *septime* is directly below quarte. You can, of course, come on guard initially in octave or septime, either with absence of blade or with engagement of blade – you will soon progress to this, either by accident as you attempt to outwit an opponent, or by design, on instruction from your coach.

32

parries for two reasons. The first is the more obvious one, that by mixing your defence the attacker will not be able to judge which type of parry you will use and so prepare himself to deceive it. Mixing the defence confuses the attacker and he can never anticipate if you do it properly. The second reason is more important – by careful selection of your defence you can prepare your riposte to greater advantage. There will be more to say of this later on

Parry and riposte – defence and offence combined

Now let us put attack and defence together. Remembering the analogy with tennis, the offensive passes from fencer to fencer with each successful parry. See again sequences 1 and 2, the first counter riposte, which is a short but complete fencing phrase. It will continue until a hit is scored (valid or invalid) or an infringement of a rule of combat. To put them together satisfactorily you must first learn to think of the parry and riposte as one move rather than two. Fencing is a very fast game and the riposte must become almost an automatic response to a successful parry.

The situation now is that we see two fencers parrying and riposting – they each have four variants of attack – direct, disengage, cut-over and counter disengage which they each meet with three parries – simple, circular and semi-circular. The same four variations in attack can, if the

fencer is sufficiently skilled, be used in riposte and counter riposte. The game at this stage is decided by players anticipating correctly or incorrectly which parry and riposte the opponent will use. Deception is already employed, most obviously in the use of the counter-disengage attack, where the attacker deceives the opponent's blade as it makes a change of engagement. With the basic moves we now possess, we can proceed further with deception, using compound attack.

Deception – compound attacks

Deception is basically elementary tactics. All sports which involve confrontation with a human opponent require a large helping of such tactics. Chess is all about tactics, about disguising the intention. In tennis, playing the ball on one side of the court and then suddenly switching the play to the opposite side, catches the opponent on the wrong foot. In rugby it is called selling the dummy. In boxing, a feint in one direction leaves the opponent uncovered and exposed to a blow in another. Fencing is very like boxing. In fencing the object of the feint is to draw the opponent's defence into one line, on one side of the body, then attack into the opposite line.

Here are examples of how it is done:

(1) You make an attack by disengage and you note that your opponent habitually uses the simple lateral parry. So you make a disengage but instead of developing it with a lunge, you use it as a feint to draw

34

the opponent's simple parry and, when he takes it, you deceive him with a second simple disengage and attack into the original line. This is called a *compound attack by one-two*. See sequence 8 – here the fencers are on guard engaged in sixte, the attacker feints of a disengage into the quarte line, the defender parries quarte and the attacker, keeping his arm straight, passes his blade under the defending blade and lunges into the line of sixte. The attack finishes in the same line in which it started.

(2) The *compound attack by double* is used on an opponent who habitually employs a circular parry for his defence. Again the attacker would start with his feint of a disengage from the line of sixte. As the opponent defends himself with a circular parry of sixte, the attacker follows the defending blade around with what we already know to be a counter disengage and develops the attack with the lunge into the quarte line. The double, therefore, starts from an engagement in one line and ends in the opponent's opposite line.

(3) The same kind of compound action would be used on the defender who makes a semi-circular parry in preference to the other two. This time the feint ought to be made into the low line because this would encourage the defender to take his semi-circular parry down into the low line; to deceive the parry the attacker raises his arm back to its normal position and makes his lunge. This is called an *attack low-high*.

35

And so one could continue, for it can easily be understood that any combination of the simple attacks will make a compound attack. It is called "compound" because the attack comprises two or more blade movements. Any one of the simple attacks, therefore, can be used as a feint to draw the opponent's parry. But, by contrast, note that the second movement, that used to deceive the parry, must correspond with that parry – in other words, a disengage (or cut-over, though we haven't mentioned this) must be used to deceive a lateral parry, and a counter disengage must be used finally to deceive a circular parry.

Stop hit and counter time

I have now covered the basic game, from which all the other progressive movements and variants can be built and related to. For the competitive beginner, however, it would seem strange to me if I omitted mention of the *stop hit* and how to deal with it. The stop hit is generally given little prominence in beginners' books and in the coaching of novices. I think this is wrong but can understand why it is so. There are two confusing paradoxes about it: technically the stop hit is the simplest of movements to perform but competitively it is difficult to know when to do it – that is the first paradox. The second paradox is that in spite of it being difficult to use properly, beginners often have an almost irresistible desire to use it.

The stop hit is a counter attack on your

opponent's attack. Let us set the scene – your opponent is over-endowed in the art of deception – compound attacking has gone to his head, as it were. He feels that by making a large number of feints he will confuse you – and so he would if you tried to follow all these feints until you picked out the final attack to parry. The answer is to stop hit – all you do is to extend the arm into the beginning of the attacking action and cut short his attack with your counter attack. To score a hit, however, it must arrive *one period of fencing time** ahead of the attacking hit. The secret of stop hitting is to read the opponent's game correctly and to anticipate his feinting before he starts.

Now it clearly takes experience to anticipate and to judge that your stop hit *will* arrive a period of fencing time ahead of an opponent's attack – so you can see why many fencing masters feel that the teaching of the stop hit should come rather late in the learning process and only when the fencer has experience. But the fact is that as a beginner you will meet novice opponents who, faced with any form of attack at all, will stop hit. Whether it's in a coaching syllabus or not, there will always be the beginner who will do it – quite often it is a more natural reaction to the attack than parrying, which takes a certain amount of

*Fencing time is the time taken by an individual fencer to execute one movement of blade, arm, body, or legs, or a combination of these simultaneously. Therefore it changes from one fencer to another.

skill. It can be used with advantage at beginner level.

So, even if *you* don't want to use the stop hit, you have got to learn about it and, more important, how to cope with it. The basic way of coping is with *counter time*. This again is simple in terms of technique (see sequence 9) – you draw from the opponent a stop hit and then you parry and riposte from it. All you have to do is make it look as though you're going to do a complicated attack with a step forward, making sure you are not so close that he can actually hit you. Being slightly out of his distance will give you time to see the counter attack when it comes, parry and riposte; it also means that you will have to lunge with the riposte.

This now completes the summary of the basic fencing movements and of why and when they fit together into the game. With this general grasp behind us we can go on to cover the detail of how to do each of the movements, how you learn to fence and how to develop your powers of deception.

38

3 The stance and attack

Much attention should be paid to the on guard position, your basic stance and how you develop your attack with your lunge – how you do them will greatly affect your progress with the other movements. They are worth looking at in great detail.

On guard

The on guard position is one of awareness, of being ready to go into action, either forward rapidly into the attack or just as rapidly backward in defence. Balance of the body and distribution of weight are of utmost importance.

It is essential to get as close to the classical position as possible, while still being comfortable – faults in stance, etc., critically affect your mobility. The position is strange and there is bound to be some discomfort at the beginning (see fig. 4).

The feet should be at right angles, the leading foot and knee pointing directly at the opponent, the rear foot pointing sideways. There should be approximately two foot lengths between them, the distance adjusted for maximum comfort. The knees should be bent equally to keep the centre of gravity low and the weight of the body evenly distributed between the feet. Here is a guide to how far the knees should be bent. Keep the body straight and look

39

Fig. 4

down, you should just be able to see the back edge of the rear foot and you should not be able to see the front foot at all. Each fencer should try this but, once again, adjust for his own comfort – this is a guide, not a rule. By flexing the legs gently, feel the balance position and the legs like springs underneath you. The hips should now be at 45 degrees to your line of fence (i.e. your leading leg) and they must remain in this position – any attempt to turn more and to efface the target will alter your foot positions when moving. Rock the body weight forward and back and get the feel of your weight on the front foot and then on the back foot. Beware of this feeling when on guard – in either of these positions you will be off balance.

Initially, the trunk should remain upright, as any leaning, especially forward, will also affect your balance. Later, when balance, co-ordination and leg strength improve, you will be able to lean slightly forward from the hips without affecting the balance, and this will assist your thrusting action when attacking.

Now for the arms. Keeping the shoulders down and relaxed, raise the forearm of the sword arm until the forte of the blade is in line with the right breast, point approximately in line with an imaginary opponent's eyes. The elbow of the sword arm should be about one hand's breadth away from the body. The hand should be held with the thumb slightly turned to the right from its normal position on top (see sequence No. 10, fingerplay). This is called *three-quarter supination. Full supination* is with the fingers facing uppermost and *pronation* is with the knuckles uppermost. Three-quarters supination ensures that when you parry, you do so with the correct edge of the blade.

You are now on guard in sixte which is the normal position for most fencers, though some prefer to fence in quarte. Rarely do fencers come on guard in septime or octave.

Now raise the rear arm until the upper part of the arm is parallel to the floor, the forearm and fingers a continuation of the

curve upwards, with the forearm pulled back slightly from the right angle position and with the fingers facing forward and hanging quite relaxed.

The left-hander is in an identical position as a mirror image of the above. The sixte position being on the sword arm side and three-quarter supination being with the hand turned slightly to the left.

The grip

You must also get this right. Future ability to manipulate the sword correctly and efficiently depends on it. Hold the sword firmly so that you are not disarmed easily and yet not so tightly that you restrict the natural movement of the handle and fingers. The detail for a right-hander goes like this: hold the sword in the left hand with the top of the blade (with the maker's name) uppermost. The handle is curved so that it will fit comfortably into the right hand. Place the thumb of your sword hand on the top edge of the handle and form a hook with the forefinger so that the first phalanx of the forefinger is on the left-hand side of the handle. The thumb should be immediately above the forefinger, with the second knuckle of the finger and the tip of the thumb touching the padding on the inside of the guard, directly above and below the handle.

See that there is no gap between the end of your forefinger and the side of the thumb – if there is such a gap it means that you are pinching the foil and this will contract the little muscle between them. As this tires so will your grip tighten and you will be unable to manipulate properly.

Think of the handle of the sword as the neck of a bird – if you hold it too tightly you will strangle it and if you hold it too loosely it will fly away.

With the thumb and forefinger in place, position the remaining three fingers on the left-hand side of the handle. Knuckles flat. The pommel of the sword should now be in the centre of the wrist (see sequence 10 for fingerplay). To manipulate the foil fast and effectively, the handle should be held with the thumb and forefinger only (the *manipulators*) and the three remaining fingers (the *aids*) should retain a light contact with the handle. The manipulators are active, the aids just stroke the handle and add authority and strength to the movement. This is called *fingerplay* and is the basis of the French school of foil.

Now too much can be made of fingerplay with the beginner, who will naturally tend to move the foil from the wrist and forearm. He must certainly be prevented from using his arm but in the early stages he ought to be allowed to forget about fingerplay – it is such a fine technique that his inevitable failure to manage it will bog him down. To do it properly take an enormous amount of practice. It is much easier for a beginner to use his wrist and, for rapid progress in general fencing correct fingerplay should not be insisted upon. The ability and urge to use the fingers develop over the whole learning life of the player, as he feels the

43

need for it.* (See page 71, under *Hitting*, for an example of where fingerplay is a real help.)

Mobility

The correct positioning of the legs is essential for maximum mobility. Whereas most fencing masters agree that individual variation is allowable and even necessary above the waist, below the waist the classic stance should admit of little variation. At the beginning it may be uncomfortable to maintain this unaccustomed position of the legs, but do try to do so as often as possible – not over long periods as this is tiring, but in short bursts with rests in between. Gradually it will become natural.

For the absolute beginner, however, the important thing is to realise what mobility is all about and to let it happen naturally, getting the feel of it. From the on guard position he must learn to move in unison with the opponent and to maintain the correct distance; he must learn to judge when he is in or out of distance. At this stage, the only important factors are that the feet be kept the same distance apart all the time, and that the front foot move first when going forward and the rear foot first when going backward.

*It may be that he will never feel the need for fingerplay. In the Italian school of fencing, the manipulation of the sword is done entirely by the wrist, so it must be efficient, given a particular general style. On the whole, however, the French school is now supreme, and is the style adopted generally in this country.

The feet are kept the same distance apart at all times to ensure that the centre of gravity is kept at the same height. If it bobs up and down it means you are expending energy and time in going up and down when you only need to go backwards and forwards. You should avoid this as soon as possible for it is not difficult and requires no special technique.

The basic action is as follows. To move forward, advance the front foot about 6 inches by lifting the toes first and placing the heel down first; as it comes to the ground, the rear foot moves up an equal distance, lifting and lowering the heel and placing the toe down first. To step backwards, the rear heel is lifted first, the toe reaching backwards. The front foot is then brought back, lifting the toe and placing the heel down first. The action should be a continuous, smooth glide over the floor the feet always in close contact with it, but not sliding, the body weight carried forward and backward over the legs and not transferred from one foot to the other.

The correct heel-toe action is so described to ensure correct balance and distribution of body weight. Providing these two factors are maintained, it doesn't do to be too exact on the heel-toe action but concentrate on making it as natural as possible.

Three things for special note

First: balance. The feet are approximately two foot lengths apart, and at right angles, with the front foot toward the opponent

45

and the rear foot turned sideways. This angling of the feet gives stability forwards and sideways and the back foot provides a base to stop you falling sideways as you move rapidly, especially during the lunge. It is worth concentrating upon.

Next, in moving, we push the body weight either forward or back, and the fencer must be able to move equally quickly in either direction, at split-second notice. Therefore his weight must be equally distributed between both feet. If you have the weight too much on the front foot you can move backwards all right, but not forwards. With the weight too far on the back foot it is the other way round.

Finally, and most difficult for the beginner; bending the knees. It is very tiring, but it is necessary and he must tone up his leg muscles accordingly. The object of bending the knees is to bring the centre of gravity closer to the floor (also assisted by the feet being apart) and so make it easier to push the body weight backwards and forwards.

What the attack comprises

The adoption of the correct fencing measure ensures that an attack from the on guard position will only reach the target if the sword arm is extended and the body thrust forward in the lunge. Let us look closely at these essential movements – you will be doing them all the time and it pays to get them right.

The extension of the sword arm should

46

come before the lunge, even if only by a fraction of a second. If the fencer's body is moving forward before the arm is straight, he is said to be *attacking with a bent arm.* There are two reasons for avoiding this: it ignores an important convention and it leaves you vulnerable. The technical weakness is as important as the convention – neither should be ignored.

By traditional convention, the attacker only achieves *right of way* by having his arm straight *before* developing the attack with the lunge. Nowadays the President of a contest will give right of way provided that the arm is straightening throughout the attack – the rule has been relaxed somewhat. But nevertheless, if two fencers attack almost together, it is the faster extension and not the faster lunge that secures the right of way and therefore the hit.

Technically, the attack will be faster and more accurate with a straight arm and the opponent will also react more to a feint – a straight arm always seems to present more of a threat than does a bent one.

Of course, when you see the expert, you cannot separate the extension of the arm and the lunge – they seem to happen together. But you must always think in terms of getting the arm out first.

Now the lunge: First, a general comment – a correct on guard stance is necessary if you are to lunge well; the centre of gravity must not be too high. The mechanical action of the lunge is as follows. By lifting the front foot the balance of the body is lost

forward and this is taken up by a thrusting action from the rear leg, until that leg is straight. At this point the front foot comes to the ground and the movement ends with the knee over the instep (see the end of the sequence pictures on counter time, No. 9; see also fig. 6). Immediately the front foot reaches the ground at the full extent of the thrust, the attack is finished and the attacker must now rebound to the recovery, back to the on guard position, where he is safe.

In learning the basic elements of the attack there is no reason why the beginner should not actually be attacking a target, be it human or a wall pad.

The attack
in more detail

Let us now look at the *development* (the extension of the arm and the lunge) and the *recovery* in more detail. The sword arm is stretched to a line slightly above shoulder level, toward the high line target of the opponent. Remember to keep the hand in three-quarter supination. The front foot glides forward, toes raised; as the balance is lost forward, the rear leg takes over and thrusts the body forward to the full extent of the lunge. The rear foot stays flat on the floor. Toward the end of the rear-leg action the rear arm drops to touch the thigh, palm facing upwards. The arm should feel as if it is uncurling, finishing as the front foot comes to the floor, heel first. The legs should arrive in the final lunge position as the point of the sword strikes the target.

48

The correct final position (see fig. 6) is as follows then: front knee over front instep; knee along the line of fence and not turned in; body upright; the sword hand, having risen throughout the attack toward the high line target and compensated for the natural body drop during the lunge, is now in line with the attacker's head; the rear arm is straight, with the back of the hand almost touching the thigh, arm relaxed; rear leg straight with the foot flat on the floor.

The recovery (see fig. 5) is started by simultaneously pushing off the front heel, bending the rear knee and raising the rear arm; this transfers the full body weight almost back to the on guard position. All that is now required is to bring the front foot back to its original position. This cannot be done slowly.* The sword arm, which is stretched at the beginning of the lunge, is kept straight during the recovery and only bends again as the front foot comes to the ground.

The lunge and recovery should not be considered as two separate movements, but, the forward momentum and the elasticity of the muscles should stimulate a *rebound* action. Remember that the prime reason for the recovery in competition is to get out of harm's way as fast as possible should your attack fail.

*A tip for practising: rock forward to the lunge and back to the recovery several times to get the feel of the leg action; then give an extra thrust off the front foot and bring it back to the on guard position, making sure that the heel comes to the floor first.

49

The lunge and recovery are strong leg actions and it is wise not to go too hard at it at the beginning. Remember always the rear arm movements down and up, as this will assist, providing the movement down is started toward the end of the lunge. The following exercises are designed to strengthen and co-ordinate the muscles of the leg.

Fig. 5

Exercise 1: Assume the lunge position. Gently stretch and bend the front leg, concentrating on pushing the weight of the body down between the legs. This exercise lengthens the muscles between the legs and helps the fencer reach his maximum limit.

Exercise 2: Assume the lunge position. Straighten fully the front leg, keeping the heel of the front foot on the ground but lifting the toe; simultaneously bend the

50

back leg, transferring the weight of the body backwards at the same time raising the rear arm. By reversing the leg action you carry the weight forward into the lunge position again. Carry out rhythmically.

Exercise 3: As Exercise 2 except that you add a little extra thrust to the stretching of the front leg and the front foot leaves the

Fig. 6

ground. Then, by thrusting off the rear leg you return to the lunge position. Perform this rhythmically, concentrating on bending and stretching the rear knee and keeping the front foot in front of the knee.

Exercise 4: Assume the lunge position. Now bring the rear foot forward to the on guard position and then revert back to the lunge. This strengthens the muscles of the front leg to take the weight of the body.

51

Faults—cause, effect and cure

We have now looked at the basic requirements for the on guard position and the
attack which develops from it. I make no
special pleading now for going on, even in
a short book, to the major faults which
weaken the performance of many fencers.
All your subsequent fencing is affected by
them so you must do your utmost to get
them right.

The boxer's front knee. We'll start with the
stance of the legs. Some fencers adopt
naturally the front knee position of the
boxing stance, though with the other leg
forward, of course. This may be all right for
boxing but in fencing the distance between
the two opponents is much greater and
consequently a greater extension of the
legs and hip joints is required. To ensure
good balance on the lunge the correct foot
and leg positions must be adopted, with
the leading knee directed toward the
opponent. The boxer's stance turns the
front knee in and balance is lost on the full
lunge (not on shorter lunges as the fencer
is not fully extended).*

The root cause is almost invariably the
hips being turned slightly too much sideways, which in turn twists the knee round,
and this is what must be looked at, rather
than the knee itself. Even if the on guard
position of the knee is correct, if the hip
position is faulty, that faulty hip will take
charge of the knee as soon as the front
foot leaves the floor, twisting it inwards.

*Beware also sprained ankles.

52

To correct the hip position is easy but requires constant practice and concentration; once a bad habit is established it feels all too natural. A good tip is to pull the front hip back a little and rotate the body slightly towards the front every time the on guard position is adopted. To find the true angle, stand with the feet at right angles and then carry the front foot forward a walking pace. When the knees are bent the hip angle of 45° must remain unchanged.

The back arm position. I believe it is essential to have the back arm in the correct classical position, or at least, to learn it correctly and then, if necessary, to modify it to that which suits personal requirements. The beginner should not use it in any way he wishes.

The fact of the matter is that inaccuracies in hitting can quite often be traced to poor use of the back arm when lunging, e.g. if the rear arm is carried out to one side, it will develop a lateral swing on its downward path and create an opposite lateral swing in the sword arm. To illustrate this – extend your sword arm and put the point of the sword in line with a target, then carry your left arm straight out to the left-hand side. Swing it horizontally to the rear and you will see that it swings your point off target. The same sort of thing happens if you do it while lunging. Remember that your essential action is forward and back – any sideways movement is *bound* to be wasteful.

If nothing is done about this fault, the fencer will, in due time, subconsciously

53

make the necessary corrections with the sword arm, aiming slightly in the opposite direction to the swing and so bringing the point back onto the target. But these two contrary swings create new faults, such as loss of balance. The only cure is to carry the rear arm in the correct position, that shown in the photograph – in a direct line with the sword arm, so that the downward action assists in the forward action of the attack and the upward assists in the recovery action back to on guard. The fault can be cured more easily by dispensing with the arm action in practice, placing the hand on the rear hip and leaving it there for the lunge and recovery. If everything else is in the right place a true lunge line will result.

Timing of the back arm swing. If the back arm is going to be used in foil fencing it must be used at the right time. If any impetus is to be added to the lunge, then the smooth, continuously firm, backward and downward swing must be made *after* the front leg action is well on its way. One could say it should be made approximately half way through the lunge but this will vary with each fencer and the point is that you must ensure that for *you* it really *is* a second stage propulsion, the rear arm taking over when the leg thrust is almost exhausted.

When it happens too early, i.e. as the sword arm is extending, it has the effect of throwing both arms in opposite directions at the same time, which obviously does not

54

help swift forward movement. Indeed, if sufficient rear arm effort is used, the fencer virtually stands still for a fraction of a second (see also *slow lunge time*).

Other minor back arm problems. These are an excessive upward swing which produces an initial upward action on the lunge (clearly wasteful) and a drooping rear arm (either untrained or tired) which produces a weak and short action downwards, usually finishing before the lunge is completed. (See *slow lunge time* for more about the excessive upward swing.)

Stiff shoulder action. The extension of the sword arm requires action from the upper arm and shoulder muscles only. The beginner uses his neck muscles as well.The give-away for this is a lifting shoulder as the arm extends. It can be tested by placing the other hand on the shoulder – as the arm extends you should feel the muscles in the shoulder move but the shoulder itself should stay still.

A lifting shoulder creates an immobile, stiff arm with slow, heavy reactions. Deceptive and evasive actions tend to be made from the shoulder and, if so, they can be picked up and spotted very easily by an opponent.

The cause is very likely to be that the sword is being gripped rather than carried, and the free movement of the wrist and forearm is being resisted. This pushes movements higher up the arm until the neck muscles are affected. You must carry and

55

not grip the sword, but this is easier said than done since, for general purposes, the arm muscles have been *conditioned* to grip. It has to be consciously avoided.

If you find that your grip is all right, then the fault probably lies in stiff shoulder muscles and you must work on loosening them up by exercises – loose shoulder shaking, shoulder rotations, loose arm swinging.

Against some strong, forceful fencers real strength may be required, perhaps all the strength you can muster, including the use of other muscles. But, in the extension, smooth action is achieved by using the minimum number of muscles – you must actively try to relax those which are not in use, for if they are tense they will slow you down.

Slow lunge time. Some fencers start going upwards before they start going forward, and no matter how hard they try their attacks are slow. This is due to faulty timing in the stretching of the rear leg. It should not start its stretching and thrusting action until after the balance is lost forward; if it starts a fraction *before* the front foot is moved, it will thrust the body weight forward over the front foot and result in a kicking action to get the front foot off the floor.

Now you might think that by kicking the front foot forward, you would gain speed on the lunge, but this is not the case. The theory of action and reaction being equal and opposite comes into play and the more effort you put into kicking the front foot forward, the more you will tilt the upper part of the body backwards, pivoting at the centre of gravity – you slow the sword arm down in its movement forward. No, the driving force for the lunge must come from the rear leg.

Stretching the rear leg before the balance is completely lost also thrusts the body weight upwards initially and gives the centre of gravity too high a trajectory, i.e an upward and forward movement rather than a forward and upward movement. Of course, a certain amount of upward thrust is necessary to compensate for the action of gravity in the forward flight, but it must be part of the forward thrust, no more and no less than is required.

For correction, plenty of practice is necessary – lifting and reaching forward with the front foot while keeping the rear leg bent. The arms can be relaxed by the sides. Once the full sense of balance lost is felt, the rear leg thrust can once again be used in the correct way.

The lifting rear foot. Invariably the beginner's rear foot ceases to remain in contact with the floor at the moment when it is most needed there – at the end of the lunge action. It does so because the weight comes off the rear foot and on to the front foot, as the momentum of the body continues forward. The rear foot is dragged forward by the weight of the body. This is serious if the attack fails and you want to get back out of range – your rear foot has come up

and that is as far as you can retreat. It may be too close for safety.

Dragging the rear foot in the lunge is not such a problem providing fencing measure is adjusted so that the full lunge is achieved and the attacker does not finish the attack too close.

Whatever you do, do not turn the rear foot over on to its side, for this has several really bad effects. The rear hip drops and tends to lock, and this makes the recovery uncomfortable; and enormous strain is thrown on to the knee joint, threatening cartilage trouble.

The lifted front heel. The toes should lift first; if this does not happen and the heel comes up first, the cause is that the body weight is shifting over the front leg before the foot leaves the floor. Once the weight is on the front leg it is *impossible* to lift the toes first; therefore the heel lifts and kicks forward, producing, as we have seen, an equal and opposite reaction backward in the upper trunk, and slow lunge time.

Bent rear knee lunge. This is a most chronic and harmful fault. The fencer never stretches his rear leg and the whole body weight is taken on the front leg. Invariably the strain thrown on the front leg results in sore and pulled muscles. The attack develops into a jump forward rather than a thrust, coupled with loss of balance forward and sideways on most attacks. Quite often the attacker finishes by falling into the opponent. Should the attack fail,

58

there is no chance of recovery and the attacker usually resorts to wild, close-quarter jabbing.

The best cure I know for all faulty rear leg actions is to place the rear foot against a wall and lunge continually, feeling the thrust against the wall. Effort is made to keep the foot there and this will ensure a stretching of the rear leg as this is the only way one can reach forward with the front foot. Eventually the impetus will be transferred to its proper place – the rear leg and foot.

4 More about basic movements

Before moving on to further discussion of what the game of fencing includes of deception, etc., you need to know more about the technique of the movements. This is as true in a book as in the process of practical learning. This chapter completes the technical grounding in the basic movements.

Defence – general

Observe any of the sequence pictures which include a parry and you will see that the only strength required to defend the target is the strength of the blade. The defender must oppose the forte of his blade to the foible of the opposing blade, the stronger part to the weaker. Then no physical effort is required. Think of your defence as a shield which deflects by a firm opposition; no attempt must be made to beat or knock the attacking blade aside. Remember that a parry not only defends the target but also gives right of way for the riposte – conservation of movement and effort in defence means speed and accuracy in riposte. Don't make your parries too hard and wide. Keep the sword hand forward (elbow about one hand's width from your trunk) and avoid the natural tendency to bring the

60

hand backward as you parry – this weakens your defence and lengthens the time required for the riposte (the sword has farther to travel).

The lateral parry

Carry the whole blade across in one piece. Moving the hand or the point first, with the rest of the sword trailing behind, makes a weak defence. A strong attack will penetrate even though the parry is well-timed.

In the sequence (No. 3) the fencers are engaged in sixte, the far fencer (A) uncovered in that line; he starts to cover the line and provides the opening for the opponent's (B's) disengage attack. As the attacking point passes A's guard, his sword moves across the body laterally, collecting the attacking blade, forte to foible, and carrying it away into the quarte line (*lateral parry of quarte*). The parry is completed when the attack is clear from the target – in this position, A's point should be about over B's shoulder. Reverse the action to parry sixte.

The circular parry

An alternative to the lateral parry on a disengage attack. In the sequence (No. 5) the attack starts in the same way as for the lateral sequence (but note that the engagement is in quarte instead of sixte) but this time A, by swinging his blade in an anti-clockwise direction, moves it under the

61

attacking blade, collecting it and carrying it back into the line of quarte. A's point again finishes over B's right shoulder. Note that A does not move his sword arm – the movement is made with fingerplay. It is clearly more economical and faster, so you see why you should aim to develop finger-play. The parry is finished when the attack is clear of the target. This is a *circular parry of quarte* (sixte would be clock-wise).

The semi-circular parry

The sequence (No. 4) shows B's attack starting in the same way as for the lateral parry but as B's blade passes A's guard, the defending blade is brought over the top, collecting and carrying the attacking blade down into the low line of octave. This parry describes a downward semi-circle with the point, first inward and then out-ward.

In some contrast to the circular parry, note that the carrying of the blade down-ward is a much firmer action and therefore the only way to do this parry efficiently is to control it with the wrist and not the fingers. But note that the forearm is stationary.

The parry is finished when the attack is clear of the front leg and A's point is approximately just inside B's front knee. This is the semi-circular parry of octave – the parry of septime finishes with the point outside the attacker's front knee.

62

Indirect attack
by disengage

In sequences Nos. 3 and 5 the attacking fencer is seen both disengaging from sixte into quarte and vice versa. The point moves in a U shape, swinging clear of the opponent's blade. This sort of attack is best done when the opponent is voluntarily moving his blade in a lateral direction or is responding to a pressure upon it. Ideally the disengagement should be made by manipulating the foil with the fingers but this is something which, as we know, will take time. Nevertheless, the beginner should concentrate upon making the movement as small as possible. This is a prime example of technical speed, for here speed is clearly related to the size of the blade movement as well as the physical effort involved. Remember that when disengaging from the opponent's quarte line into his sixte, the point must be lifted over the opponent's sword arm. Thus the point has a down, up, down path whilst moving continuously forward. This contrasts with the movement from sixte into quarte, where the point may be slipped through, the opponent's arm not being in the way.

Indirect attack
by cut-over

This is a wrist action with a firm opposition to the opponent's blade, though without creating too much lateral movement. There are two ways in which it can be done: either by *lifting* the blade over the top or by

63

withdrawing the arm slightly. The French school favours the latter, because the foil is a thrusting weapon and by withdrawing the arm the point is kept down and in line with the target. It may be thought that speed is lost in bending the arm backwards but, in actual fact, at fencing measure, the amount of backward movement required is negligible.

Look now at sequence no. 6, where they are engaged in quarte with A, the facing fencer, uncovered in that line. As A attempts to cover his line with a lateral movement, B withdraws the sword arm slightly. Note here that he pronates the hand (fingers down): this exerts added pressure upon A's blade, encouraging him to move his blade a little more laterally than he would desire – this makes the cut-over more effective and gives B that extra time needed to get to the target, needed because of his withdrawn forearm.* B must keep the point in front of the guard all the time, for the action must maintain the character of a thrust (see *Hitting*, page 71) Having negotiated A's blade, the arm must now be straightened, turning the hand back into its original three-quarter supinated position, for otherwise the attack may well be inaccurate. He must beware here, too, making a bent arm attack, the tendency being to lunge whilst the arm is bent instead of when it is stretching.

Most fencers become used to disengage

*B would *supinate* the hand if they were engaged in sixte (fingers uppermost) – why the difference?

attacks and the cut-over becomes successful because of its surprise, particularly when the defender makes a mistake in fencing distance and comes too close.

Indirect attack
by counter disengage

This gives fencers the most trouble in learning and is also often forgotten in competition. The reason is possibly that only the most controlled fencers move their blades in true circular movements and therefore the beginner gets little practice.

It is the type of fencer who covers his line with a change of guard that you attack by counter disengage. You create the situation by pressing on the blade, or you wait for him to take a change of guard. When it comes, you follow the circular movement around, passing under the opponent's blade and coming back into the same line in which you started.

The essential points about the movement are that (whether you employ fingerplay or not) it is kept small, relating this to technical speed again, and that it is not started too early, which is what most beginners do. Delay your movement until the opponent's blade has already passed under your own, i.e. until the last possible moment, just before the contact of the change of guard. Practice it in fairly slow time on an opponent, so that you get the feeling of starting a fraction of a second before his change of guard is completed. When this movement is done at full speed

65

it is only a feeling of timing, not a calculation.

As the names imply, disengage and counter disengage clearly have some connection, and this can help you fix their characters in your mind. Let us compare the directions in which the blade moves in these two movements. From the on guard enaged in sixte your blade would move from left to right if you wish to attack by disengage; but if you attack by counter disengage you would wait until the opponent starts his change of guard and you would deceive by moving from right to left, i.e. the other way.

But both the disengage and the counter disengage must be executed in one progressive, forward motion and should be visualised as a spiral movement towards the opponent's target (different to the cut-over). Both, when finishing in the line of the opponent's sixte, must be carried over the opponent's sword arm, so both require a slightly exaggerated lifting of the point before striking the target.*

*Note also, and it is forgotten by beginner and more experienced alike, that all these simple attacks can finish in the low line, under the opponent's blade or defensive action. In such cases, remember that the hand should be fully supinated if the attack finishes in the line of septime but pronated in the octave. This ensures that the blade, when fixing upon the opponent's target, bends laterally, so that there is no chance of the bend of the blade catching up in the opponent's sword arm. Supination or pronation is effected throughout the whole of the attack.

66

The riposte

This is an offensive action which follows a successful parry. It can be, as with the attacks, simple or compound. Although the parry and riposte are essentially two separate moves, one defensive and the other offensive, they must be integrated, as you cannot riposte without successfully parrying. But clearly, if you develop the parry and riposte to a stage of completely automatic action, you will be vulnerable when your first parry is deceived. Therefore, although the fencer must build up a spontaneous response in the parry and riposte, and a natural reaction to parry if his attack fails, sufficient control and timing must be exercised to allow his play to fit that of his adversary. Automatic action is easily dealt with by a competent swordsman.

Thus, a direct riposte will often be parried (see sequence nos. 1 and 2 – first counter riposte) and the riposter must resort to indirect or compound ripostes. These have similar techniques to the corresponding indirect and compound attacks, with the following differences:

First – Because the attacker is now very close, the deception of his parry, whilst he is on the lunge, must be made with a bent arm. To stretch the arm too soon results in a miss or a hit off target. The arm must be extended after negotiating the attacker's parry. Anxiety to score a hit causes the riposter to stretch his arm too soon.

Second – Again, because he is so close, the attacker will react automatically to your

67

parry, so the riposter, anticipating which parry he will use must deceive immediately with his indirect riposte, and not make a feint, as he would for an attack. Example: Two fencers are on guard engaged in sixte; one attacks by disengage and the defender successfully parries with a lateral parry of quarte; the attacker, realising his attack has failed, will respond with his own lateral parry, whilst still on the lunge, expecting a direct riposte. The defender, anticipating this, swings his blade under the moving blade of his opponent and hits him in the line of sixte (this riposte would be a disengage), i.e. instead of feinting to draw his opponent's parry, as in attack, he *anticipates* the parry.

Third – When making a riposte by cutover, the backward action of the arm must be slightly exaggerated, in order to clear the opponent's blade. Again, the attacker is nearer now.

Fourth – When riposting with a counter disengage, it is the timing which is important. The initial tendency is to move too soon and so the beginner should make himself wait in the parry position until the final part of the attacker's circular parry before attempting his deception. Remember, too, that the arm is stretched at the end of the movement.

Here are two more useful general tips about riposting: (1) Any movement other than a direct one is bound to lose time – if the attacker is fast and reacts to your parry, he may be able to recover to guard and this will give him time to respond. (2) Remember that the size of a riposte by disengage must be relative to the blade and arm it deceives – it can be just as disastrous to make the disengage too small and get caught up on the opponent's sword arm, as to make it too large, which slows the move down.

Compound attacks

I will first analyse the sequence for the one-two compound attack (no. 8) and describe briefly once again the double and the attack low high.

The *one-two* refers to the fact that it comprises two disengagements. Sequence 8 shows an engagement in sixte, with the attacker (A) covered. The opponent (B) attempts to cover his line with a lateral movement. On this, B disengages his blade and extends his arm, threatening the quarte line. B defends himself with a lateral parry, but A has anticipated this. He maintains a straight arm and deceives the parry with a further disengagement (using the fingers and making the movement as small as possible), lunging and delivering the attack proper in the sixte line.

The *double* comprises a feint of a disengage attack, anticipating that the opponent will defend with a circular parry, which you deceive by following his blade round and then lunging into the opposite line to the original engagement. The attack *low-high* is a feint of a disengage into the low line, underneath the opponent's sword arm. He tries a semi-circular parry of

69

octave, which you deceive by disengaging your blade back into the high line.

In fact, the four basic attacks can be combined in many ways. Much practice in mental agility can be found in trying various combinations from various starting positions. Let the defender take pre-arranged combinations of two parries and the attacker fit his compound attack into them. Go slowly at first; even so, the attacker will move in the wrong direction many times, though he knows his opponent's defence.

Further points to observe: (1) Note that there is no necessity for compound attacks to deceive the parry in the precise manner we have described. It is possible to make a feint into the high line and instead of deceiving the parry completely the attack is passed underneath it. Conversely, if the feint is in the low line and the parry is taken into the low line, then the attack itself passes over the top of the blade. (2) The attacker's arm is stretched at the beginning of the attack and the arm is maintained in this position throughout the whole length of the attacking move. (3) The deception of the opponent's parry must be only sufficiently large to get around the opposing blade and sword arm. (4) The smaller the movements the faster they are in terms of technical speed. (5) The development of the attack by lunging must be made at the precise timing of the opponent's parry. Ultimately it will be found that the whole attack of two blade movements can be developed throughout one lunge so the attacker may even be

70

lunging at the beginning of the first move. However, this requires a high degree of co-ordination and a beginner would be better advised to keep the lunge to the second part of the compound attack.

Hitting the target

For the beginner the hit seems an obvious thing, but he will soon find himself missing the target and hitting the sword arm, which will seem constantly in front of it.

The act of hitting is described in many technical books as the "placing of the point on the target, with the fingers", i.e. finger-play. The average beginner will, of course, aim with the wrist or the arm. Fingerplay need not, indeed should not, be insisted upon, but it is important to eliminate the use of the arm. The reason is clear – by using the arm one tends to lose speed, either by making forward movements with it or by bending it in the middle of an attack. Moreover, it is important that the attacking movements remain within the confines of the target, i.e. that they continue progressing forward once on route towards it. Arm movements wave the point about and attacks are inaccurate. Therefore you must quickly train yourself to use only the wrist as a beginner. You can fence efficiently with it.

The advantages of using the fingers will become clearer as you proceed. As your anticipation and technical control improve, you will realise you are like a football team with excellent potential midfield but with

71

no-one in the forward line who can shoot goals. To hit accurately you must develop a feeling of *where your point is*, i.e. you must instinctively know what you must do at any time to bring your point back into the line of an accurate attack. You must be able to *cast* it at the target, from wherever it may be, rather like a fisherman casting a fly on the water. Striking the target is not just a mechanical action, stretching the arm – the extension of the arm with the lunge are subsidiary factors to the need to place the point first. It is well worth spending a lot of time in front of a small wall pad, on the lunge, practising hits from close quarters and at all sorts of angles.

The bent arm

This keeps creeping into almost every fencer's game. The more anxious a player is to score a hit, the faster he will try to deliver it. This tempts him to move his leg first (the heavier limb) and his arm second – hence a bent arm attack.

To control the bent arm is a psychological problem, for in such cases it is the result of stress. The only way I know to *cure* this is to take the pupil completely out of the competitive environment for a long time and to re-train the arm and leg co-ordination from scratch. Nobody likes this. The best way to *prevent* it is correct, persistent training at the beginning. This is easier said than done.

72

5 **Deception**

During the learning of the elementary fencing phrase you will very likely practice by having one fencer agree to start the attack and each fencer then parries and ripostes according to an agreed pattern. This helps the technical learning of the moves but is also a very good exercise for developing rhythm in your fencing. It is probably your first introduction to what is called *cadence*, which is the adjusting of your fencing time to that of your opponent's. In the early, practice stage, this has the character of a metronome timing and it is interesting to see how long two fencers can keep it up.

Even at this practice stage you will notice that your opponent naturally has a different rhythm of movement to your own. Whether an individual's rhythm is fast or slow is not, within the normal bounds, a particularly significant factor. The faster is not necessarily the more effective, for someone with a swift rhythm may well be more easy to deceive – he may well be too fast, off before he knows where he's going to. (Remember again that fencing is technical as well as physical speed.)

Now right from the beginning it is important to learn to adjust your rhythm to that of your opponent. You should learn to control your own natural rhythmic inclination, to make it flexible. The reason for this is simple – if you can adjust your

rhythm to suit your opponent's, you can also *change* your rhythm to gain an advantage. Adjusting rhythm to an opponent is the first simple example of analysis we have met. It is one of the simplest and most important aspects of the art of assessing your adversary's game.

Now the obvious way in which being able to change your cadence is advantageous, is suddenly to speed up. You are riposting and counter riposting and the regular rhythm of the phrase lures your opponent into a false sense of security – a sudden turn of speed may well break through his defence. This is a simple case of deception. But there is a less obvious and more intriguing way, which is to *slow down* the cadence.

Broken time

In the last chaper I remarked that the cut-over possessed an element of surprise and I can now suggest a reason for this which is more interesting than the fact that it is a less performed movement than the similarly purposed disengage. I have mentioned that the cut-over attack virtually has no loss of speed when compared to the disengage, as the amount of arm withdrawal is so slight at fencing measure. But in the riposte by cut-over, the arm withdrawal is considerably greater, owing to the closeness of the attacker.

This exaggerated arm action does produce a slowing down of the fencing rhythm and this can have a most interesting result.

Quite often the cut-over riposte hits in the *same line* as the parry, instead of the opposite line as it should. This is because the attacker has taken his parry at the normal cadence and has been *too fast*. The cut-over causes a break in time, or cadence. This is a simple example of what is called *broken time*. Expert fencers use this deliberately to deceive.

Now this concept is closely linked to compound attacks. First, I should point out that these can be made in three basic sorts of time: *two-time* is when the attacker makes the feint from the on guard position and then makes the second, deceptive blade movement on the lunge (this is how beginners should start); *progressive* is when the two blade movements are fitted into the whole lunge, i.e. the whole compound attack is a spiral toward the target (this is used against one who fences in normal rhythm); *broken time* is a variation upon a normal progressive attack. It is where the feint is made with an almost complete lunge and the second, deceptive movement made as the front foot comes to the floor. This is made on one who holds his parries to the last moment. It is difficult and I personally am convinced that it ought not to be *taught* to a fencer, but that it should develop naturally. Broken time is a *sense* of timing which develops through experience in fighting.

But, as a beginner, you should understand what broken time is about. I shall try to suggest where you should start your experiments with it.

75

The right time to attack

But I am going to lead back to broken time from another, simpler aspect of deceptive fencing, namely when you should attack, how you should *time* your attack.

There is a right time and a wrong time to attack and this can be put very simply by saying that the right time is when the opponent is not able to use distance to his advantage and is therefore forced to parry your attack. Right at the beginning of the book I pointed out that much tactic was concerned with fencing measure. What I am saying here is that the right time is when the opponent has little ability to alter the measure, he cannot move away from your attacking blade. We are concerned with the action of gravity on the body as he steps forward. When the opponent makes the initial movement of the front foot in the step forward, it is impossible for him suddenly to change his mind, at that split second in time, and to move backward. He *must* complete the first action of the front foot before he is able to change direction and go the other way. Consequently, if the correct fencing measure is observed, he cannot get away from the attack by putting distance between himself and your point.

Now you should learn not to *wait* for the opponent to make this movement forward but, by varying your footwork rapidly and anticipating that if you step back your opponent will step forward, you should try to control time and distance, so that you launch the attack that fraction *ahead* of your opponent's step forward.

76

This is an important point, to which we shall return, namely that you attack when the opponent has committed himself. For the moment we will consider another, similar example of vulnerability and link this one up to the changing of cadence, to broken time. The example here is that the opponent has attacked you and you have successfully parried, but you have decided not to take up the right to riposte, but to hold the parry. You wait for the opponent to move away from you with the recovery.* During the time of the recovery the opponent is anchored to the ground by his rear foot and is most vulnerable (he is also that much closer, which enhances the speed of your attack). Do not confuse such an attack with the riposte, because the pause creates a new situation – the attack is taken up by *you* on the opponent's recovery. In order

*A successful parry gives you the *right* to riposte – you do not *have* to. Should you hold the parry, and decline the riposte, you are almost saying, "Look, it's my turn but I abandon it – go on, you make another move". The opponent can do two things, he can either retreat or he can attack. He retreats with his recovery; he attacks with a *renewed attack*. There are three types of these – the Remise, the Redoublement and the Reprise. *The Remise* is a renewed attack in the same line as the original attack – i.e. a direct renewed attack. You could use it against an opponent who holds his parry and opens the line again to your attack. *The Redoublement* is an indirect or compound renewal, i.e. you can't score in the original line, so you disengage or cut-over into another line. A *Reprise* involves recovering to on guard by moving back or bringing the rear foot forward. It can be like a recovery in the initial move.

for this to be read as a parry and riposte the riposte must follow *continuously* from the parry action.

This example resembles the former in that you attack when the opponent is committed to moving his weight from one foot to another. But it also brings us back to cadence, for what you do here is to break the rhythm – introduce a pause. Now this can mentally jolt the opponent. He may well dither over his recovery, contract upon himself. But note again that you have to be able to do it properly. You must control the parry and be able to wait that crucial split-second whilst he commits himself to recovery; and you cannot delay long or he will be back on guard. You have to attack *at the right time*. This is really something you *feel* inside you.

I have suggested that you should experiment with attacking when you sense that the opponent is in some sense immobile, without options in his movements. I suggest now that you also concentrate on such times as when your opponent is *mentally* immobile. It should by now be clear that during combat the mind is turning over patterns of attack and defence and counter-attack all the time. These patterns will be confused from time to time – after a movement which has failed; when moving mentally from an attacking to a defensive attitude; when moving forward aggressively in preparation for an attack. In short, when the mind is switching in some way or other.

Let me put it the other way – the *wrong*

time to riposte is when an opponent is making half-hearted or probing attacks, preparing the way for a full attack. At such times he is at a distance where he can normally react and cope with the situation. You must wait until he is fully committed: when he has delivered an attack fully, tried to score. It may be that in order to achieve this you must feed him with a riposte or two to bring about his complete commitment.

Reaction time

What you are doing when you catch him physically or mentally unaware is to put him in a position where he is unable to react with control to your move – he moves without premeditation. That people take time to react is common experience. There is the game I am sure everyone has played where a pound note is suspended between the thumb and forefinger – it is yours if you catch it before it drops. This is impossible, unless you are able to anticipate, since the pound note will drop before you are able to react to the fact that it has been released. Catching an opponent unawares is to trick him so that his normal reaction time is slowed.

Let us look at this reaction time a little more closely for it will reveal something implicit in all our talk about catching the opponent off-balance – namely that when under pressure an opponent will react *automatically*.

If, as an experiment, you stand so close to an opponent that you can hit him on

79

target simply by extending the sword arm, then engage him in sixte with the opponent fully covered in the sixte line (i.e. so that you can only hit him with an indirect attack); and if you attack with a disengage, you will see that the opponent is unable to parry, for you are moving within his re-action time. Of course, you must do the attacks properly: if your disengagement is too large you will lose speed, and if you make a series of disengagements to a regular rhythm, the defender will not be parrying when he sees the beginning of your movement but will be parrying to a set rhythm, and will succeed.

But if you take care of these two points, the attack should arrive almost every time, even though he knows that it is going to be a disengage. If you extend the distance slightly he will be much more successful. At full fencing measure such a forewarned disengage has no hope of success.*

*These sort of exercises are good practice. Here is another. Stand at riposting distance, where you can reach your opponent by extending the arm; both fencers on guard in sixte, fencing with absence of blade. The attacker must try to score a hit on the opponent's target by making a beat direct attack (a *beat* is a sharp tapping action made on the opponent's blade. It has two purposes: either to knock the sword aside and give you way for a direct attack or to make the opponent react in such a way that you can deceive the reaction and thereby launch an attack). You must not use the legs. On the beat from the attacker the defender must try to parry quarte. It will be found that an attack rarely fails if the minimum amount of effort is used for the beat, and if the attacking movement is truly direct.

80

Now the point is that when, by timing your attack carefully, you seem to be about to outpace your opponent's reaction time, he will tend to do that which he instinctively feels will work. He must do something or he is lost and he has no time to think.

Second intention

Observation of an opponent can tell you what his instinctive reaction to such a situation would be (incidentally, it is very likely to be a lateral parry) and much deception in fencing turns on playing upon such weaknesses. This is called *second intention*. Any compound attack is an example of second intention. You observe that an opponent habitually takes a particular parry (even when under no pressure) and so you make a feint to draw that parry. Again, if you know that an opponent takes a particular parry and riposte, then you attack him, not with the intention of scoring a hit but of allowing him to parry and riposte. You are prepared for that riposte and follow with a planned counter-riposte.

This is where the analogy with chess is clear but I think I ought to mention now where it is that this analogy breaks down. In chess there are many clever people who can think two, three or even more moves ahead of an opponent – I have never met them in fencing. The reason is that there are factors involved other than thought and analysis, namely speed and technique. These may let you down. Therefore you

81

should not try to be too clever – once a movement fails, regardless of what it is, you have to fall back onto the fencing phrase, the ability to continue on from the present unpremeditated situation, disregarding your previous premeditation.

And, furthermore, should your action succeed, what is the point of trying to out-think your opponent *again*. This is an important point. Since the object of deception is to make an opponent defend in one direction whilst the attack or riposte moves in the other, it is tempting to think that the more deceptive movements the better. This is not so. The more movements you make, the more time there is for the defender to see and size up the situation. One cancels out the other. A fencer, therefore, and not just the beginner, should limit himself to two (sometimes three) blade movements – if unsuccessful, he should try another approach. By two blade movements I mean the two disengages of the one-two.

The stop hit

If you do try a more complicated attack, such as a one-two-three, you may very likely be subjected to a stop hit, for this elaborate sort of deception can be very smartly dealt with by that method. Perhaps the stop hit has little of deception about it. Actually to deceive an opponent into letting you stop hit him is difficult. But there is much to say about when to use it and when not to use it.

Let us look first at when not to use it.

Since your hit has to arrive a period of fencing time ahead of your opponent's, it would be fatal to try one on someone who jumps in with a straight arm and point in line. The swords and arms being approximately the same length mean that you will hit each other at about the same time, in which case the hit will be scored against you since his was the original attack. It will also not work against an opponent who does progressive compound attacks, with both blade movements executed on the lunge, since this will also be regarded as a single period of fencing time.

Therefore the real chance of success is against someone who habitually attacks with a bent arm (if your arm is straight he will impale himself on your blade), against a fencer who does compound attacks in two time, and against one who tries a large number of feints in the hope that he will confuse you. You should study *where* you can hit the opponent on target, by studying his attacking movements. Such a sudden attack must be directed into a line which is at least going to be open throughout the attack's initial stages. Note also that you can deliver what is called a *stop hit in opposition*. This is where you anticipate the final line of an opponent's attack, extend your arm in that line and deflect the final part of the attack itself, his sword sliding along in opposition to your own, being deflected as it goes. This is clearly only possible when you are able to anticipate his final attacking line and can see that he is uncovered in your own attacking line.

83

The stop hit cannot be used indiscriminately and you will probably only get away with it once or twice. The best time to use it is after you have been playing a defensive game. But having been successful with it, expect your opponent to be a little more wary next time and be prepared for him to switch from compound to simple attacks. It is advisable to fall back on defence before trying it again.

Do not rely on the stop hit, for it tends to inhibit the development of the other movements. It is no substitute for the parry. Against an evenly matched opponent, it requires excellent perception, control of distance and quick reactions.

Counter time

This is all about deception: it is a prime example of second intention. Counter time is where you draw a stop hit from the opponent with the premeditated intention of parrying and riposting from it. What you are doing is saying to him, "Look – I am doing a complicated attacking movement. Stop hit me – that's the right move to make"; then you parry the stop hit and score with the riposte. See sequence 9.

This invitation to attack comprises a series of blade movements or one emphatic blade movement, which is normally coupled up with an emphatic foot movement like the *balestra* (a jump forward which is normally followed immediately by the attacking lunge). You've got to jump forward because the opponent isn't

84

going to stop hit you unless he really believes he is going to be attacked – the blade movement alone is not really sufficient. The jump forward needs precise judgement, for it must be of such a length to give the opponent the feeling that he can reach you when, in fact, he can't – a matter of inches. If you do jump too far you've had it – there is no escape, he will hit you if his timing and speed are good. But once he is committed to the stop hit, he is at your mercy if your judgement is right.

Clearly, if you jump forward and are not so close that he can reach you, then you're not so close that you can reach him. This means you may have to lunge with your riposte. How far you lunge is dependent on how close you are. It should also be clear that a direct riposte has generally little chance of success, if you have to travel a fair distance. It is very successful at close quarters but not so successful if you have to lunge (that's why indirect attacks are needed, after all). So, with counter time, you must anticipate the opponent's reaction once his stop hit has failed, and make an indirect or even a compound riposte (a one-two in sequence 9).

Assessing the adversary

Put quite simply, the art of deception depends first on probing and understanding your adversary's game, and then having the technical ability to exploit the weakness you discover. By and large, your intention is to hustle the opponent into an automatic

parry, an automatic reaction. You hazard that if you do such-and-such he will do so-and-so. You do not *know* he will do this but you take the chance – a calculated risk. He can perhaps fool *you* into thinking he is vulnerable.

You find out how the opponent parries by peppering him with a series of simple movements. Few good fencers take the same parry every time so you can expect him to change his defence pattern. You must find out what his defence pattern is, which parry he will change to and when. There are some intriguing generalities – on the whole a fencer tends to change his defence every third movement – this is no more than a generality, but it is something to be going on with. You, in turn, must try to make your pattern of defence and attack such that it can't be recognised. You must look for bad technical habits and try and disguise your own. Everyone has faults and bad habits. To even pre-suppose that any system of training will eliminate all bad habits is to expect a machine and not a human being to perform. In my 20 years as a coach I have watched people at Olympic level win gold medals with all the bad habits in the book.

You should also assess the general character of your opponent. Broadly speaking there are two types of fencer: he who fences by pure reaction to the external conditions, i.e. to what you present him with, and he who works out a plan of action and tries to control you.

86

Absence of blade

This book has concerned itself with fencing with blades in engagement, because it has been the most convenient way for me to explain the game to you. In fact, most competitive fencing is with absence of blade and I will end with some words about this. Nothing in the book loses its value because of this, for you are still concerned with the basic attacks, ripostes and parries, and the framework of deception into which they fit.

Like tennis, where base-line play has yielded to service and volley power in the modern game, so have swift footwork, judgement of pace and distance, speed and aggression, superseded elaborate conversations with the blade in modern competitive fencing. This is why absence of blade is prevalent. Failure to maintain the correct fencing measure after an attack has failed or as an attack is to be mounted, is something you must therefore watch for in an opponent and guard against it yourself. There will be much stepping forward and backward and, as we have seen, fencers are vulnerable at such times. Feet come too close together, causing unbalance, some fencers rush to and fro without meticulous care of footwork – such movements are uncontrolled and the fencer is particularly vulnerable to the stop hit.

Absence of blade has affected the initial blade movements in attack. Feints must be made to induce parries, either high or low; if and when the opponent responds, then

87

the attack follows as usual for the compound attack. Hits with direct attacks are rare, due to the increased fencing measure.

One fencing convention needs commenting upon further. If you extend your arm in line with the target, the opponent must remove your blade before he can launch an attack, for you have established a right of way. He must use *beats*, *pressures* and *prises de fer* (taking the blade). By observing which type of movement he will use on your blade, you can be prepared for it, parry and riposte from it. Although hits with direct attacks are rare, such attacks can be used by you as feints to lay traps. They encourage beat or prise de fer attacks, which you can parry and riposte.

These attacks on the blade occur frequently when fencing with absence of blade. They are necessary in order to draw reactions and movements from the opponent. They are not things which can be easily discussed here, for there is little technique in them – they are largely concerned with deception, with anticipating how an opponent will react to each particular beat or pressure.

They open up further horizons in your fencing and provide both a just ending to this book and a starting point for experiment.

APPENDICES

Equipment

The foil: This must be selected wisely, and properly balanced and set. If it is bought at a shop where the assistant does not understand fencing, you must subsequently have it balanced to suit your own individual requirements.

Check that the foil is put together properly. Hold it in your left hand at the widest part of the blade, nearest the guard, handle towards you. The manufacturer's name should be stamped on one side and the blade size on the opposite, just where it enters the guard, No. 5 is the normal size for adults; No. 4 is approximately half an inch shorter, and is mostly used by young people. It has a smaller, lighter handle (ask for a *junior model*). Hold the sword with the manufacturer's name uppermost. This is called the top of the blade. In this position the handle should have a fairly straight left edge but the right edge is shaped to fit into the palm of the hand (right-handed). The reverse will apply for a left-handed sword. If set correctly, the handle will now be sloping slightly to the left and downward from the guard (to the right for left-handed). Now place the forefinger of the left hand under the blade about one inch from the guard. The sword will approximately balance at this point. My personal

view on this is that the sword should be slightly point-heavy. This means that so balanced the point should drop slightly. If the sword is very point-heavy you can counter-balance it by unscrewing the pommel and inserting in the base one .22 shot or fishing weight. One rarely gets a sword which is pommel heavy but if this is so it is adjustable later on, when the blade breaks, get a slightly heavier blade.

Blade flexibility: Check the flexibility and look to see that it's not too thick, especially at the forte, and see that there are no flaws in the steel. A blade which is too *soft* is poorly tempered and sooner or later will not spring back into its original line. A blade which is too rigid or too *hard*, will break quickly. To find the right temper, press the point of the sword against the floor – it should feel lightly springy.

Handles: There are two types of French handles – corded or leather covered. The corded is slightly cheaper but my advice is to buy the leather covered. It feels much better. The leather is a *tacky leather* – it will never polish and become slippery. The National Training Scheme of Great Britain is based on the French style of foil play and it is an advantage to have the correct handle. The Italian School sword has a cross bar attached to the handle. There are few Italian-based clubs. The other type of handle used today is called an orthopaedic handle. There are many varieties of these and they're usually made of metal and shaped to fit into the hand rather like a pistol grip. Some coaches allow their pupils to use such handles, but my advice is to start with the classical French handle and learn the French School. The only main reason, as far as I can see, for using an orthopaedic handle is that you have a weak hand or you're not physically able to manipulate the classic French foil. There is an argument that strength of grip is required today as the game is more athletic and much faster and stronger. But if the game is learnt properly and the art of deception and evasion applied, I don't see that this is a valid point. I most certainly have not found it necessary to change my handle. However, the choice of handle is purely an individual one.

Protective clothing: Most fencing clubs provide equipment, so beginners can see what they need to buy when they join. The essential clothing for a beginner is a mask, a jacket and a glove. The masks are made in several sizes, so make sure that you pick one which fits your head. The jackets can be bought made-to-measure or off the peg and any glove will do to start with so long as it covers the opening of the sleeve of the jacket. Special chamois leather fencing gloves are made. One can buy fencing trousers and fencing shoes but a pair of track suit trousers, especially the stretch nylon type, will be sufficient for the beginner. Any shoes used in the gymnasium will be adequate. .

Safety precautions: Fencing is not a dangerous sport providing liberties are not

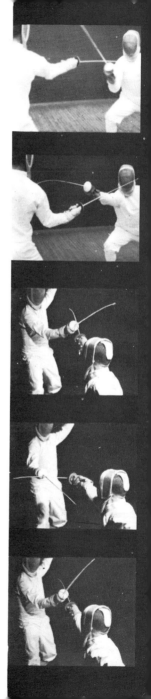

91

taken with the normal safety precautions. Here is a list of them one should remember:

1. Never fence without a mask.

2. Make sure the point of your sword and, more important, your opponent's sword, is covered. The manufacturers provide plastic buttons which fit over the point of the sword.

3. If participating in *free play*, always wear a jacket and make sure that the jacket adequately overlaps the trousers. Jackets are made specially for left-handers or right-handers and you should make sure that the buttons of the jacket are away from your sword arm side. Some jackets are made with a zip up the back. Ladies' jackets are available with breast protectors.

4. The glove must always cover the opening of the sleeve of the sword arm.

Fencing clubs

Most towns and cities in this country have a fencing club or an evening class run under the Further Education Authority. The Central Council of Physical Education (CCPR) have many offices, and information of classes and clubs may be obtained from this source. The governing body of fencing is the Amateur Fencing Association which maintains a full list of all classes and clubs in this country. Information can be obtained from:

The Secretary, Amateur Fencing Association, De Beaumont Centre, 83 Perham Road, West Kensington, London W.14.

92

CCPR Regional Offices

North-East: 40 Saddler Street, Durham City. Tel.: Durham (0385) 4278/9

Yorkshire: 2 Park Square East, Leeds LS1 2NQ. Tel.: Leeds (0532) 36443/4

North Midlands: 26 Musters Road, West Bridgford, Nottingham NG2 7PL.
Tel.: Nottingham (0602) 81325/6 & 89102

East: 5a Harpur Street, Bedford. Tel.: Bedford (0234) 50181.

London and South-East: 160 Great Portland Street, London W1N 5TB. Tel.: 01-580 9092.

South: Watlington House, Watlington Street, Reading, Berkshire RG1 4RJ Tel.: Reading (0734) 52342 & 57740.

South-West: 17 The Square, Crewkerne, Somerset. Tel.: Crewkerne (0460 31) 3491.

West Midlands: 52 Frederick Road, Edgbaston, Birmingham 15. Tel.: Edgbaston (021 - 454) 3808

North-West: Ralli Building, Stanley Street, Salford M35. Tel.: Blackfriars Manchester (061 - 834) 0338 & 9573.

Northern Ireland: 49 Malone Road, Belfast BT9 6RZ. Tel.: Belfast (0232) 669519.

Wales: 47 Cathedral Road, Cardiff CF1 9UH. Tel.: Cardiff (0222) 31546/7.
Divisional Education Offices, Abbotsfield, Rhosddu Road, Wrexham. Tel.: Wrexham (0978) 3404.

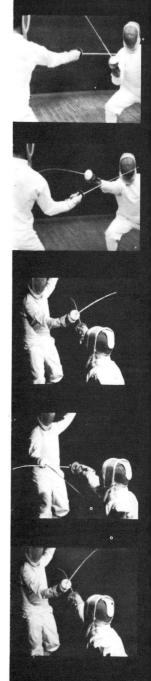

Flick backwards